EVERYTHING

GABRIEL JOSIPOVICI was born in Nic̶̶̶̶̶̶̶
Romano-Levantine parents. He lived ⸺ ₒ/ ꜰ ꜰrom 1945 to
1956, when he came to Britain. He read English at St Edmund
Hall, Oxford, graduating with a First in 1961. From 1963 to 1996
he taught at the University of Sussex, where he is now Research
Professor in the Graduate School of Humanities. He has
published over a dozen novels, three volumes of short stories
and a number of critical books. His plays have been performed
throughout Britain and on radio in Britain, France and
Germany, and his work has been translated into the major
European languages and Arabic. In 2001 he published *A Life*, a
biographical memoir of his mother, the translator and poet
Sacha Rabinovitch (London Magazine editions). His most
recent novels are *Goldberg: Variations* (Carcanet, 2001) and *Only
Joking* (Zweitausendeins, Germany, 2006). In 2006 Carcanet
published a collection of his essays, *The Singer on the Shore*.

Also by Gabriel Josipovici

Fiction
The Inventory (1968)
Words (1971)
Mobius the Stripper: Stories and Short Plays (1974)
The Present (1975)
Four Stories (1977)
Migrations (1977)
The Echo Chamber (1979)
The Air We Breathe (1981)
Conversations in Another Room (1984)
Contre Jour: A Triptych after Pierre Bonnard (1984)
In the Fertile Land (1987)
Steps: Selected Fiction and Drama (1990)
The Big Glass (1991)
In a Hotel Garden (1993)
Moo Pak (1995)
Now (1998)
Goldberg: Variations (2002)

Theatre
Mobius the Stripper (1974)
Vergil Dying (1977)

Non-fiction
The World and the Book (1971, 1979)
The Lessons of Modernism (1977, 1987)
Writing and the Body (1982)
The Mirror of Criticism: Selected Reviews (1983)
The Book of God: A Response to the Bible (1988, 1990)
Text and Voice: Essays 1981–1991 (1992)
Touch (1996)
On Trust (1999)
A Life (2001)
The Singer on the Shore: Essays 1991–2004 (2006)

(ed.) *The Modern English Novel: The Reader, the Writer and the Book* (1975)
(ed.) *The Siren's Song: Selected Essays of Maurice Blanchot* (1980)

GABRIEL JOSIPOVICI

Everything Passes

A Novel

CARCANET

First published in Great Britain in 2006 by
Carcanet Press Limited
Alliance House
Cross Street
Manchester M2 7AQ

A CIP catalogue record for this book is available from the British Library

ISBN 1 85754 850 7
978 1 85754 850 1

The publisher acknowledges financial assistance from Arts Council England

Typeset in Monotype Centaur by XL Publishing Services, Tiverton
Printed and bound in England by SRP Ltd, Exeter

For

Marianne Fillenz

and

Stephen Mitchelmore

A room.

He stands at the window.

And a voice says: Everything passes. The good and the bad. The joy and the sorrow. Everything passes.

A room.

He stands at the window.

Silence.

He stands.

Silence.

He stands at the window.
   Cracked pane.
   His face at the window.
   Greyness. Silence.

And again the room.
   The window.
   He stands at the window.
   Silence.
   He turns from the window.
   He begins to pace.
   The empty room. The bare boards.
   The sound of his footsteps on the bare boards.
   He stops at the window.
   He stands.
   Greyness. Silence.
   He stands at the window.
   Silence.

Again the room.
  The window.
  He stands.
  The cracked pane.
  Grey light.
  He stands.

And again the room.
  The window.
  He stands at the window.
  A knock at the door.
  He turns.
  The knock is repeated.
  He waits.
  Facing the door, he waits.
  The door opens. It slowly opens.
  It is his son.
  He stands in the doorway.
  He says: —So.
  He closes the door behind him, stands with
his back to the door, looking round.
  He whistles. —So, he says again.
  —Have a seat.
  His son laughs.
  —You like it?

3

—Like? his son says. Like?

The window. Cracked pane. Grey light.

His son advances across the bare boards. His footsteps echo on the bare boards.

He stands next to him at the window. Runs his finger over the crack in the pane.

—So, he says, for the third time.

—Don't.

—Why?

—I don't like the noise.

They stand side by side, looking out.

—Well well, his son says.

And again the room.

The window.

He stands at the window.

Greyness. Silence.

He stands.

And a voice says: Everything passes. The good and the bad. The joy and the sorrow. Everything passes.

A grandfather clock: tick *tack* tick *tack* tick *tack* tick *tack*.

Thick curtains on either side of the French window.

That smell.

Her smell.

— Why are you holding the door open? he asks.

She giggles.

— Why?

She giggles.

— Go on, she says.

The clock: tick *tack* tick *tack* tick *tack* tick *tack*.

Her smell.

— Go *on!* she says, stamping her foot.

— You want me to go through? he asks.

The clock: tick *tack* tick *tack* tick *tack* tick *tack*.

— Do you?

That smell. *Her* smell.

He steps past her through the French window.

And again the window.

His face at the window, looking out.

The cracked pane.

Greyness. Silence.
His face at the window, looking out.

Sunlight.
The garden.
She walks beside him on the grass, between
the flowerbeds.
Sunlight.
Silence.
They walk.
They walk.

The room.
He stands at the window.
Greyness. Silence.
The crack in the pane.
Behind him, the phone begins to ring.
He turns from the window, crosses the room.
His footsteps on the bare boards.
He picks up the receiver. He says — Yes?
Nothing.

He puts down the receiver, returns to the window.

Greyness. Silence.

The cracked pane.

His face at the window.

Silence.

The garden.

He stands.

She stands beside him.

—Go on, she says.

He begins to walk again. She walks beside him.

The room.

He stands at the window.

The cries of the children in the playground below.

He stands.

Behind him the phone rings.

He turns. He crosses the empty room. He picks up the receiver.

—Dad? his son says.

—Yes?

—Are you all right?

—Of course. Why?

—You sound funny.

—Do I? he says.

—How are things?

—What things?

—Have you had anything to eat today?

—Of course.

—I'll try and come round tomorrow, his son says. I've got a lot on.

—I'm fine, he says. There's no need.

—No no, his son says. I'll be round. OK?

—There's no need.

—See you tomorrow, his son says.

He puts down the receiver, walks back to the window.

He stands.

Grey light. The cracked pane.

The cries of the children in the playground below.

He stands.

The garden.

He runs on the grass between the flowerbeds.

The sun on his face. He runs.

Behind him, her laughter.

The sun on his face.

He runs.

His daughter goes from room to room, opening the windows.

—Where are you sleeping? she calls out.

—How do you mean?

—The bed hasn't been slept in, she says. Are you sleeping on the couch?

—Yes, he says. I think so.

—What do you mean you think so? Don't you know?

She stands in the doorway. —Don't you know? she says again.

—I sleep where I find myself when sleep falls upon me, he says.

—Come on, Dad, she says. Stop trying to make me feel sorry for you.

—I didn't ask you to come.

—That's not the point, she says.

He sits in the kitchen while she cleans the

house. He can hear the vacuum cleaner in the
bedroom over his head.

He sits. He waits for her to leave.

His face at the window.

Greyness. Silence.

The crack in the pane.

His face at the window.

Silence.

Sunlight.

The garden.

The shuttlecock flies into the bushes.

—I can't! she says. I can't play any more!

—You want to stop?

—I want to lie down, she says. I'm sweating all
over. I want to lie down with you in the grass.

The room.

He stands at the window.

Behind him, the phone rings.

He turns from the window. He crosses the room, his feet echoing on the bare boards.

He picks up the receiver.

Nothing.

He puts down the receiver, returns to the window.

His face at the window.

Greyness. Silence.

His face at the window.

And again the room.

He stands at the window.

The cries of the children in the playground below.

In the distance, the hum of city traffic.

Behind him, the phone rings.

He lets it ring. It stops.

It starts to ring again.

He crosses the room, picks up the receiver.

His daughter says: — Why didn't you answer?

— When?

— Just now.

He waits, holding the receiver to his ear.

—Dan called me, she says. He says he just spoke to you and you sounded low.

—No, he says. I'm not low at all.

He waits.

She says: —Dad?

—Yes?

—Do you want me to look in?

—No, he says.

—It's no trouble. If you'd like to see me.

—No, he says. There's no need.

—Are you sure?

He waits.

—Are you sure? she says again.

—Thank you.

—Dad?

—Goodbye, he says.

He holds the phone away from his ear. He can hear her voice. She says: —Goodbye, Dad.

He puts down the receiver. Walks to the window. Stands.

His face at the window.

The children's cries mingling with the hum of distant traffic.

The living-room with the bay window.

Between them, the draughts board.

—Can I take it back? he asks.

—No, she says. Once you've touched a piece you can't take it back.

—All right.

—But then I gobble up all three pieces, she says, laughing.

—What can I do? I touched it.

—And then, with my two queens, she says, I can gobble up these as well.

She moves her queen swiftly over the board, collecting his pieces on the way and piling them up at the side.

—I saw you, she says.

—What?

—I saw you at the bedroom window.

—What do you mean? he says.

—You were looking at me sunbathing, she says. You were looking at my naked breasts.

The board. His hand.

—I don't mind, she says. It's perfectly natural. We are cousins, after all, aren't we?

The board. His hand.

—Aren't we? she says.

I want to go out, his son says.

— That you shall, he says.

— Oh, Dad, don't speak like that.

— How do you want me to speak?

— Let's go now, Dad, his son says.

— No, he says. Not now. Wait till Mummy comes home.

— Please, Dad.

— All right, he says. But it's raining. Do you really want to go out in the rain?

— It's just a few drops.

— It's more than that.

— It'll be over by the time we get out. Dad. Please.

— All right. Put your coat on.

Outside, he says: — Put your hood up.

— It's hardly raining.

— You know how easily you catch cold. Put it up.

— Don't fuss, Dad, his son says.

They walk in single file because the pavement is up.

— Are we going to the park? his son asks.

— Yes.

— Hurray! his son says.

Where the road-works end his son is waiting for him and takes his hand. — I don't like the rain, he says, do you?

— Not much.

14

—Is Mummy going to be there when we get back?

—Perhaps.

They enter the park.

—Can I run? his son asks.

—Yes. Off you go.

His son runs, waving his arms.

His daughter goes through the house like a whirlwind, opening and shutting windows, dusting and vacuum cleaning.

He sits in the kitchen, waiting for her to finish.

Finally, she is done.

She stands at the sink, washing her hands.

—Do you want some tea? she asks.

—All right.

As she makes the tea she says: —Come on, Dad. You've got to pull yourself together.

—Why? he says.

—You've got to. For her sake.

—What's she got to do with it? She's dead.

—You know she'd have wanted that, she says.

—How do you know what she would have wanted?

—Oh, Dad, she says.

—They drink their tea.

—How you loved her, she says.

—Yes, he says.

—Much more than Mother, she says.

—I loved your mother.

—Not in the same way.

—She let me down.

—Oh, Dad, she says. Will you never understand?

—No, he says. Apparently not.

The garden.

Sunlight.

He runs down the grassy path.

—Wait! she says. Wait for me, please!

He stops, panting.

She stands beside him.

—Come, she says. I want to lie down. I want to lie down with you in the grass.

The room.

The window.

He stands at the window.

And a voice says: Everything passes. The good and the bad. The joy and the sorrow. Everything passes.

—Rabelais, he says, is the first writer of the age of print. Just as Luther is the last writer of the manuscript age. Of course, he says, without print Luther would have remained a simple heretical monk. Print, he says, scooping up the froth in his cup, made Luther the power he became, but essentially he was a preacher, not a writer. He knew his audience and wrote for it. Rabelais, though, he says, sucking his spoon, understood what this new miracle of print meant for the writer. It meant you had gained the world and lost your audience. You no longer knew who was reading you or why. You no longer knew who you were writing for or even why you were writing. Rabelais, he says, raged at this and laughed at it and relished it, all at the same time.

—Will you write about Rabelais? she asks.

—Yes, he says. I think so. I want to tell people about his modernity. About what he means or should mean to all of us, now.

He looks at her. She smiles.

The room.

He stands at the window.

Greyness. Silence.

He stands.

—Rabelais, he says, is the first author in history to find the idea of authority ridiculous.

She looks at him over her coffee-cup. — Ridiculous? she says.

—Of course, he says. For one thing he no longer felt he belonged to any tradition that could support or guide him. He could admire Virgil and Homer, but what had they to do with him? Homer was the bard of the community. He sang about the past and made it present to those who listened. Virgil, to the satisfaction of the

18

Emperor Augustus, made himself the bard of the new Roman Empire. He wove its myths about the past together in heart-stopping verse and so gave legitimacy to the colonisation and subjugation of a large part of the peninsula. But Rabelais? If enough people bought his books he could make a living out of writing. But he was the spokesman of no one but himself. And that meant that his role was inherently absurd. No one had called him. Not God. Not the Muses. Not the monarch. Not the local community. He was alone in his room, scribbling away, and then these scribbles were transformed into print and read by thousands of people whom he'd never set eyes on and who had never set eyes on him, people in all walks of life, reading him in the solitude of *their* rooms.

— Do you want another coffee? she asks.

— Yes please.

When she returns he says: — And yet the funny thing is that he wants to do nothing other than scribble away in his room.

She slits a packet of sugar and pours it into her coffee.

— Why? he says. What was it that drove him in this way?

— Haven't writers always written alone in their rooms?

— Of course, he says. Ever since writing was

invented. But even if Chaucer wrote alone in his room we know he read what he had written aloud to the court. Dante no doubt composed in the quiet of his study, but, like the stonecarvers of the cathedrals, he devised his work first and foremost for God. And, from the beginning he wrote his poetry to be performed in public. In the *Purgatorio* he imagines an old poem of his being sung back to him by his musician friend Casella on the shores of the Mountain of Redemption:

Amor che ne la mente mi ragiona
cominciò elli allor sì dolcemente,
che la dolcezza ancor dentro mi suona.

He is silent, looking down at his coffee.

—Didn't other writers of Rabelais' time feel the same as he did? she asks.

—Perhaps they did, he says. But it doesn't show in their work. The poets still wrote for each other and for their patrons. Shakespeare wrote for an audience he knew and could see every day. Rabelais invented modern prose fiction. And no one really understood what he was up to for the next four hundred years, except for a few kindred spirits like Cervantes and Sterne. I want to make our culture aware of what he sensed and how he responded to the crisis of his time, which is also the crisis of our time. I want to sweep away the popular image of Rabelais as a writer of bawdy stories and nothing else. I want to make people aware of the issues he faced and so clear the ground for a genuine renewal of fiction writing in our day.

— How did it go again? she asks, looking him across the table.

— What?

— The Dante.

— Love that discourses in my mind (that's the first line of his old poem), he then began so sweetly that the sweetness still within me sounds.

He smiles at her: — *Che la dolcezza ancor dentro mi suona*, he says.

The room.
   The window.
   He stands at the window.
   Greyness. Silence.
   He stands.

And again the room.

His son.

—So, he says, this is where you live.

—Yes.

He walks to the window, looks out.

From the playground below, the sound of children playing.

—What's this? he says, pointing.

—The crack?

—You should get it replaced, his son says.

—Yes.

—But you won't.

—No.

—Because you're cussed?

He takes a walk round the room.

—How long has it been like this? he asks.

—I don't know.

—You don't know?

He resumes his tour of the room.

—You don't know? he repeats. Was it like this when you came?

—I think so.

He stops, facing him. —What is this, Dad? he says.

—What?

—What are you trying to prove?

—Prove?

—Living like this. What's it supposed to prove? That we don't love you?

—No.

—Then what?

—Nothing.

His son strays to the window again, runs his finger along the edge of the broken pane.

—Look, Dad, he says, it makes me feel bad, your living like this.

—I'm sorry.

—But you won't do anything about it?

—No.

—Dad, his son says, don't cut yourself off from us. We love you.

He moves to the door. —OK, I'll go now, he says. Take care.

He closes the door carefully behind him.

His feet on the stairs.

The children's cries from the playground below.

A table.

—For Shakespeare, he says, sipping his coffee, the old ways still held. It's true that there was a new relationship to the audience, it paid hard cash at the entrance now instead of lining the streets to watch the festival carts go by. Sal, he says, how long have we known each other?

—Six months, she says.

—Sal, he says, will you marry me?

—Yes, she says. Of course I will.

—Good, he says, I hoped you'd say that. Shakespeare's audience, he says, paid for the privilege of entering an enclosed space to watch and listen to a play. But it was still an audience he could see, an audience every segment of which he knew intimately, he had drunk with them all, with the bargemen and the chandlers and the barbers and the soldiers, he had attended on the lords and ladies, he was on first-name terms with the aldermen and Justices of the Peace. His words went out to them and their applause came back to him. But with Rabelais it was different. He was not a popular playwright but a writer of prose fiction. But what was prose fiction? What were its rules and parameters? What was the nature of its pact with its new audience? You know, Sal, he says, I knew you'd say that the first time I set eyes on you.

On the swings his son says: —Daddy! Daddy!
Push me! Push me harder!

He holds his son's narrow shoulders, pulls
him towards his chest, then releases him into the
void.

—Higher, Daddy! Higher! Higher!

His son rises up into the sky.

He helps his son undress.

—Where's Mummy? his son asks.

—She's gone away.

—When will she be back?

—I don't know.

—When, Daddy?

—I told you. I don't know.

—Liz says she's gone for good.

—Perhaps she has.

—Why, Daddy?

—Perhaps she doesn't like us any more.

—Why, Daddy?

—Perhaps we're not very likeable.

—Why, Daddy? Why?

And again the room.

He stands at the window.

And a voice says: Everything passes. Never fear. Everything passes. The good and the bad. The joy and the sorrow. Everything passes.

The kitchen.

A table.

He says: — You can divide the writers of the last hundred years into those who've understood and those who haven't. It's as simple as that. Into those who have grasped what Rabelais was up to and those who will never grasp this, no matter how long they live and how often you explain it to them. What I like about your work, Brian, he says, is that you've understood. Everything else about it is flawed and weak, but that doesn't matter. It's early days. You will change and grow. The other thing you either have or you don't. And you do.

— Am I supposed to thank you for that? Brian asks.

— No. To take heart from it.

The kitchen.

—I like it, he says. I like the fact that it doesn't so much begin as simply appear, not so much end as disappear. I like that very much.

—That's what I was after, Brian says.

—We are hardly aware of it and then suddenly it's there in front of us. We are hardly aware of it and already it's starting to vanish. That's good.

—I worked very hard for that, Brian says.

—It doesn't show.

—I'm glad you think so, Brian says.

—Supper's ready, Sally says.

—You'll stay?

—Thank you, Brian says. I'd love to.

When she has done cleaning the house his daughter makes the tea.

She says: —There's no need to think about these things now.

—I'm not.

—Give it time, his daughter says.

—Time?

—Oh, Dad! she says.

She brings the pot to the table. — You may find, she starts.

— Please, he says, holding up a hand.

She kisses him. — I'm going now, she says.

— You're not going to have any tea?

— I can't. I need to get back.

— Yes, he says.

— You'll be all right?

— Yes.

— I'll call in tomorrow. But ring if you need anything.

— Yes.

He hears her get her coat and leave.

He sits in the empty house.

— The trouble with most works of literature, he says, is that they face you head on. It's never like that in real life. Things just slip past us and we're hardly aware of them before they've gone. You know what I mean?

— Your food, Felix, Sally says.

— Can I finish what I was saying?

She is silent.

— Damn, he says. I've lost the thread.

They eat.

—Very good, Sally, George says.

—That, Brian says, is what I tried to do, at any rate. I wanted it to be something seen out of the corner of the eye, so one's not sure one's even seen it. I don't know if I managed to bring it off, but that's what I was after.

—Oh you have, you have, he says.

They eat.

—Sterne knew that living one's life isn't like sitting in the theatre and watching a play, he says. And then it was forgotten till Virginia Woolf killed Mrs Ramsay off in a bracket.

—Actually I was thinking of Byron, *Don Juan*, Brian says.

—More, George? Sally says.

—I can't resist, George says.

—More? Sally asks.

—No thanks. Did I ever show you that piece I did on round and square brackets in *To the Lighthouse*? he asks Brian.

—Was it in that collection Tony edited?

—You remember it?

—Of course.

—I know you're not wild about Woolf, he says. I don't think I am. But she was on to something. She had the courage to explore, and of how many writers can that be said?

—Brian?

—A little, please.

They eat.

—Pass your glass, he says to Brian.

—Thanks.

—George?

—Please.

—What's for dessert? he asks.

—Your favourite, Sally says.

—Ah, he says. You spoil me.

—All right, he says to his son. We can go home now.

—Oh, Dad!

—Liz'll be waiting.

—Let her wait.

—That's not very nice, is it?

—All right, Dad. Just one more.

—One more then. Are you ready?

—All the way back, Daddy. All the way back.

—Hold on tight then. Here goes. Whuuuuuupsie!

Hand in hand they make their way back across the park.

In the study Brian sits facing him.

—Why? he says.

—It felt right, Brian says.

—It doesn't feel right to me.

—What's wrong with it.

—Too elegant.

—That's what I was after, Brian says. Elegance.

—Remember Stevens' quip about Arp?

—Tell me.

—'The human spirit has little to fear from him.'

—Meaning?

—You're pandering to them, Brian. A little fear is essential to good art.

—One can't turn it on.

—True.

Sally puts her head round the door. —You'll eat with us? she asks Brian.

—Thank you. I can't be other than I am, he says.

—I'm asking you to be yourself.

—That's what I am, Brian says. That's me.

—Pity, he says.

As they wash up he says to Sally: —They're all the same. They can't go through with it.

—What do you mean?

—English writers, he says. They're all the same. Self-indulgent. Sentimental. And an eye on the main chance.

—You're hard on him, she says.

—George doesn't think so.

—George! she says.

—They're all the same, he says.

—You're too absolute, Fee, she says. It's inhuman.

—On the contrary, he says. I say what I do because I believe in the man.

—That's not the same as being human.

—Does being human mean not having standards any more?

—You're too hard on him, she says.

—Perhaps it's because I think there's something worth saving.

—Perhaps you should be a little more flexible, she says.

—There isn't anything to be flexible about, he says. There's the truth and there are lies, that's all.

—What makes you think you have a monopoly on the truth?

—I don't. I just think if I believe something's bad I have a duty to say so.

—It's only your opinion, she says.

—I hate that phrase, he says. If everything's only an opinion everyone can do what they like.

—What gives you the right to decide you know the answer? she says.

—I have to believe it, he says, or life's not worth living.

She scrubs, rinses. He dries.

—He writes too much, he says.

—He may feel you write too little.

—I only write what I feel has to be written. He listens to his agent and his publisher and his publisher's publicist and God knows who else and out go his standards.

—No, she says. His standards are your standards, Fee. You know that.

—He's the best young writer I've come across, he says. I don't want to see him go to the dogs.

—He won't, she says. Not with your belief in him.

—It's wearing thin, he says.

He walks with Lotte through the art gallery in Munich.

—You know, he says, I've often dreamed of walking through an art gallery with you.

—And now your dream has come true, she says, laughing, rubbing up against him.

That smell. Her smell.

—I don't know what to do with it now it's come true, he says.

—You don't do anything about it, she says. You just do it.

The room.

He stands at the window.

Greyness. Silence.

His face at the window, looking out.

—Why do you keep buying this plain yoghurt? he says. You know I can't stand it.

—The doctor said—

—I don't care what the doctor said. You

know I don't like it. I won't eat it. Do you understand?

She is silent.

—Do you? he says.

—You don't want him to succeed, do you? she says.

—What are you talking about?

She is silent.

—Why do you do it? she says finally.

—You're asking me to defend myself?

—No. Just to think a little.

—What is there to think about?

—You're undermining his self-confidence, she says. Do you realise that?

—Why are you standing up for him? he says. Why do you defend him against me? I've given him everything.

—He's frightened of you, she says. He's frightened of the power you exert over him. He feels the need to shake free of you.

—What power? he says. What are you talking about?

—What's the matter with the two of you? their daughter says.

—Keep out of it, Liz, he says.

—I will, she says, and leaves the room.

—Don't talk to her like that, Sally says.

—And you don't talk to me like that in front of the children. Understood?

—Do you know how *you* talk to *me*? she says.

—Oh come on! he says.

—You should hear yourself some time, she says. You should hear yourself talking to me about yoghurt.

—Yoghurt? he says. What has yoghurt got to do with it?

—You didn't hear how you talked to me about yoghurt?

—The woman's mad, he says. First Brian and now yoghurt.

—You don't hear yourself, she says. He feels he won't survive in your shadow.

—What shadow? What are you talking about?

—I'm talking about the effect you have on people.

—I say what I think, he says.

She is silent.

—He's no good, he says. He's no better than the rest of them. He's disappointed me.

—You? she says. What do you have to do with it? What's important is that he shouldn't disappoint himself. Why do you always have to see it in personal terms, as a slight to *you*, a feather in *your* cap? When will you begin to understand that the whole world doesn't revolve around you?

—And I won't eat this yoghurt, he says. Is that understood? Doctor or no doctor. I want

raspberry yoghurt. Or peach and mango
yoghurt. But not plain. Not low fat. I can't stand
low fat. It's nothing but milky water. I won't
have it. Is that understood?

His son sits with him in the cluttered living-
room. — Everything is going to change, he says.
— Yes.
— You're going to be terribly lonely.
— I'll manage.
His son cracks his knuckles, as he does when
he is not at ease. — In a way, he says, death is
easier to bear than the other.
— What are you talking about?
— You know.
— You're talking about your mother?
His son cracks his knuckles again. — I'm
sorry, he says. Perhaps I shouldn't have said that.
— You must say what you think.
His son looks down at his hands.
— If you want to go, he says.
His son stares at the floor.
— Don't worry about me. I can take care of
myself.
— No, his son says. All right. He gets up.

They go to the door together.
They embrace briefly.
— All right, his son says. Take care.

The room.
    Greyness. Silence.
    The phone.
    It echoes in the empty room.
    It stops ringing.
    Greyness. Silence. The empty room. The bare
boards. The phone. The window.
    The cracked pane.
    Greyness. Silence.

The kitchen. The table.
    — Where's the coffee? he says.
She doesn't answer.
    — Where's the coffee? he says again.
    — There, she says. Right in front of you.
    — It's decaf, he says.
    — That's right.

—Where's my coffee?

—That's it, she says. There.

—No it's not. It's decaf.

—That's what the doctor says you should have.

—I'm not interested in what the doctor says. I want my coffee.

—I want to talk to you, she says.

—I don't want bloody decaf, he says. I want my own coffee. If you won't buy it then you can at least tell me so that I can buy it myself. She is silent.

—What about? he says at last.

—Us, she says.

—Us? he says. What about us?

—Fee, she says. I'm leaving you.

—What?

—I'm leaving you.

—What do you mean you're leaving me?

—I'm going to live with Brian.

—What?

She is silent.

—I can't believe this, he says.

—We're in love, she says.

—In love? he says. He's half your age.

—Don't exaggerate, she says.

—I can't believe this, he says. I can't believe what I'm hearing.

—Brian and I are in love, Fee, she says. I'm leaving you for him.

—In love? he says. Do you think you're in a film or something?

She is silent.

—Sal, he says gently. People don't just walk out like that in real life.

She is silent, looking down at the table.

—How long has this been going on? he says.

She is silent.

—I can't believe I'm hearing this, he says.

—I have to, Fee, she says.

—What do you mean you have to?

—You don't know the effect you have on people, she says. You don't listen to anything except your own voice.

—My own voice? he says.

She is silent.

—And when are you planning to do this? he asks.

—Now, she says.

—And the children?

—They will come with me.

—I don't think so, he says.

—You're going to make difficulties?

—You bloody well bet I'm going to make difficulties, he says.

—I see, she says.

He is silent.

—I thought I should tell you, she says. Rather than just going.

—I see, he says again.

—Leaving a note, she says.

He looks at her. Then he says: —Well? Why don't you go then?

—Yes, she says. I'm going.

The room.

He stands at the window.

And a voice says: Everything passes. The good and the bad. The joy and the sorrow. Yes. Everything passes.

The park.

The swings.

And his son saying: —Higher, Daddy! Higher! Higher!

—Hold on tight then!

—Go on, Daddy! His son shouts. Send me up into the sky!

Send me up into the sky.

The room.

From the playground below, the cries of the children. In the distance, the hum of city traffic.

He stands at the window.

Behind him, the phone begins to ring.

He crosses the empty room and picks up the receiver.

His daughter says: —I wondered if you needed anything. I could bring it round today.

—No, he says. No. I don't need anything, thank you.

—OK, his daughter says. Ring me up if you change your mind.

He says: —Thank you. He replaces the receiver.

He stands.

The room.

He stands.

Lotte.

That smell. Her smell.

She says: —So I came back.

—To this, he says.

They watch the rain come down.

—I heard, she says. I'm sorry.

—How?

—I heard.

They stand.

—And the children? she says.

—I see them, naturally, he says. But not as much as I would like. And now everybody feels awkward.

—I never wanted children, she says. Charlie said he didn't either, but now he accuses me of depriving him of them.

—He accuses you?

—You know how it is, she says.

And again the room.

He walks up and down, up and down. He walks.

He stops at the window.

His face at the window.

In the distance, the hum of city traffic.

His face in the grey light, looking out through the cracked pane.

Lotte.

—He rang one day, she says. He said he was bankrupt. Why do you have to tell me that over the phone? I said to him. There is nothing left, he said. No house. No furniture. Nothing in the bank. Nothing. I couldn't understand why he hadn't waited till he got home to tell me. Why he had to phone from the office to tell me. I can't come home, he said. I can't face you now I'm bankrupt. What do you expect me to do? I said. Go to your mother's, he said, that will be the best. I'm not going to see you again? I said. I can't face you, he said. Can't you understand? Now that I'm bankrupt I'm too ashamed to face you. Go to your mother's, he said. That will be the best. Then he put down the phone. I packed my bags. I never liked the house. I never liked Washington. I don't think I ever liked him. I packed up my bags and came back. Now he is on his feet again and has another woman.

They stand at the window and watch the rain.

—But still, she says, he accuses me of never having borne him a child.

—And the other woman?

—He says he is too old now to cope with children. But still he accuses me.

They watch the rain.

—Does that make you sad? he asks.

—What?

44

— That you never bore him a child?

— Children frighten me, she says. I never wanted children. I wouldn't know what to do with them.

They walk through the art gallery in Munich.

— I remember when you teased me as a boy, he says.

— I teased you?

— Mercilessly.

— How?

— You flirted with me, he says. You teased me.

— I didn't.

— I was obsessed with your breasts, he says. That year you came to stay with us. I would have given anything to touch your breasts.

— Why didn't you?

— I was afraid of your reaction.

— Perhaps I wanted you to touch them.

He is silent.

He says: — You sunbathed with your breasts bare, knowing that I was looking from the bedroom window.

— Poor Felix, she says. He is silent.

—I'll make up for it now, she says.

— Will you? he says. Really?

— Of course, she says.

The room.

The window.

He stands at the window.

The fourth movement of Beethoven's string quartet, Opus 132.

He presses the switch. The music stops.

He gets up. He goes out into the garden.

Sunshine.

Lotte.

He reaches out an arm and touches her.

— Hullo, she says.

— Hullo.

She straightens and turns.

Sunshine. The garden. He smiles.

— I like your garden, he says. I like your house.

—It's your house too now, she says.

—I feel at home here.

—I'm glad, she says.

—Perhaps I can even begin to work again here, he says.

—Good, she says.

—I mean real work.

—I know, she says.

And again the room.

He stands at the window.

And the voice says: Everything passes. The good and the bad. The joy and the sorrow. Yes. Everything passes.

The first movement of Beethoven's string quartet, Opus 132.

A knock on the door.

—Yes? he says.

The door opens, it slowly opens.

George.

— Lotte told me to come straight through, he says.

— Good to see you, George.

He switches off the music.

— And you, George says.

He looks round: — Am I disturbing? he asks. Lotte told me to come straight through.

— No no. I was dozing. I can't seem to do much, these days.

— I'm not surprised, George says.

— Coffee?

— No, George says. Don't bother. I just called to see how you were doing.

— And what do you find? Felix asks.

— You look good.

— I do?

— Sure, George says. Considering.

— What was it the man said? Acute perception of mental blunting. Final paradox.

— Give yourself a break, George says. They thought you'd died, for Christ's sake.

— I thought so too.

— How do you mean? George asks.

— I'll tell you about it some time.

— No, George says. Tell me now.

— Not now. Some time.

And again the room.
    He stands at the window.
    Greyness. Silence.
    He stands.

—I thought I had died, he says. I felt my heart
stop. I thought I had died.
    — Tell me about it, George says.
    — Not now. Another time.

The room.
    The window.
    The cracked pane.
    Greyness. Silence.
    His face at the window.

—I had woken up in the night, he says, filled with such dread I hope never to feel like that again. But when I awoke in the morning all that had passed. Instead I was filled with a kind of euphoria, a sense of wellbeing and excitement such as I had never felt. It seemed to fill every part of my body, from the tips of my toes to the top of my head. I couldn't wait to sit down at the desk. It felt as though at last I would be able to say it all. Say everything. Everything. Such joy.

—I was at my desk, he says to George. Bent over the sheets of white paper. A neat stack of them. Such whiteness. Such paper. I was writing fast, without pause, setting down on the white paper what had been waiting all those years to come out. Everything would be said. I knew that. Everything. I couldn't write fast enough. All in the right order. It was coming out in the right order. I knew it was the right order. I just knew. It flowed out of me. I couldn't stop.

—Everything, he says to George, who nods and strokes his moustache. I was putting everything down. So clearly. So beautifully. That's how it began.

The room.

He stands at the window.

And the phone begins to ring.

He crosses the empty room, picks up the receiver.

—I almost rang off, his son says. Where were you?

—Here, he says. At the window.

—You had the pane fixed?

—No.

—Why not?

He is silent.

—Why not, Dad? his son says. Be sensible.

—Yes, he says.

—Do you want me to get hold of a glazier for you?

—No.

—You won't do anything about it?

—No.

—Fuck you, Dad, his son says.

He is silent.

At the other end of the line, his son waits.

He puts down the receiver.

— All those years with nothing to say, he says to George. Or no way of saying it. And then suddenly I could say it all. It was so easy, he says to George, who strokes his moustache and nods, nothing has ever been so easy in my life. It flowed out of me like water. And yet it wasn't easy. I knew I had to concentrate. I knew I wouldn't be given a second chance. My hand hurt but I knew I couldn't stop. Not till it was done. All done.

He stops.

— Do you want to rest? George says.

— Yes.

— I hope I haven't exhausted you.

— Of course not.

George gets up. — I'll call Lotte, he says.

He tiptoes to the door, stops, looks round.

— I'll call her, he says. Good man.

The room.

He stands at the window.

Greyness. Silence.

He stands.

—Like water, he says to George. Yes. Like water.

—I don't know how long I remained, bent over the page, he says. But it was a long time. A long time. I wondered if I would be able to hold out. If my fingers would be able to stand it. But of course they did. I did. Till it was done.

—I stopped, he says. I closed my eyes. I was exhausted. Triumphant but exhausted. As if I had finally done what I had been put in the world to do.

—I bent my shoulders, he says to George, who nods and strokes his moustache. I bent my shoulders and let my arms hang down. I stayed like that for a long time. A long long time. And then I opened my eyes and began to look over what I had written.

—The page was black, he says. It was black with marks. Thick with them. Nothing was legible. And the page underneath was white. With the traces of writing from where I had pressed on the page above. And the traces gradually disappeared as I turned one page after the other, until there was nothing but whiteness. Pure whiteness. Page after page.

—I hadn't turned the page, he says. Not once. All the time I was writing. I hadn't turned the page.

—That's how it began, he says.

The room.
The window.
Greyness. Silence.
He stands at the window.
He stands. In the silence. In the greyness.
He stands.

—I knew I had died, he says to George. I could
feel the needle going through my heart. I knew I
had died.

—That was the injection, George says. Your
heart had stopped. They had to revive you with
injections.

—It was a red-hot needle, he says. Going
through my heart.

—Your heart had stopped, George says.
Something had to be done.

—Red-hot, he says. Right through. I knew I
had died.

—Two or three times, George says. They
had given up hope, but the injections got it
going again.

The room.
  The window.
  His face at the window.
  Greyness. Silence.
  His face at the window.

—I saw a door, he says. An opening door. I
wanted to go through that door.
  He is silent.
  —And then? George says.
  —I knew if I had long enough I would be
able to go through that door.
  —You could see through the door? George asks.
  —No. But I knew everything would be all
right. If I went through.

—I saw myself standing in an empty room, he
says. I was standing at the window, looking out
through the cracked pane.
  —Then I saw my face at the window, behind
the cracked pane. Looking out.

He is silent.

—Behind me, greyness, he says. Greyness and silence.

—Your heart had stopped, George says. That's why they gave you the injections. To get it going again.

—I knew I was dead, he says. And I knew if only I could get through that door all would be well.

—All would be well, he says. Better than it had ever been. Yes, he says. Better than it had ever been.

The room.

He walks up and down, up and down, his footsteps echoing on the bare boards.

He stops at the window.

He stands.

He begins to walk again, up and down, up and down.

He stops at the window.

He stands, looking out.

His face at the window.

Greyness. Silence.

His face at the window.

— I could see myself in the empty room, he says
to George, who nods and strokes his moustache.
I could see myself at the window.

— Sometimes, he says to George, my feet
echoed on the bare boards. Sometimes there was
only silence. Greyness and silence. Inside the
room and out. Greyness and silence.

— Sometimes, he says, I could hear the cries
of children in the playground below, and
sometimes I could hear the distant hum of city
traffic. But most of the time there was just
greyness and silence, greyness and silence, and
my face at the window, looking out.

Lotte.

They walk through the gallery in Munich.

— My God, he says to her. Do you see that girl?

— What girl?

— In that picture, there.

— That one?

— Yes.

— What about her?

— It's you, he says.

— Me?

— As you were when you teased me in the garden.

— When I—?

— Who's it by? he says.

They approach the picture and he reads out loud: — Danae. Jan Grossaert, gen. Mabuse, 1478–1532.

— You really think so? she says.

— Yes, my darling, he says. It could be you. Even now it could be you.

His daughter goes through the house, cleaning, cleaning.

He sits in the kitchen and waits for her to depart.

She stands at the door. — There, she says. That's better.

She comes into the kitchen. — Have you

thought about what you're going to do? she asks.

—No, he says.

—There's no hurry, she says.

—No, he says.

—Well, she says, I must be off now. I'll call again in the next day or two.

—There's no need, he says.

—You'll be all right?

—Yes, he says.

—All right then, she says. I'll be off.

He hears her go down the corridor. Then the door opens and shuts and she is gone.

The room.

Music: the fourth movement of Beethoven's string quartet, Opus 132.

The movement comes to an end.

Silence.

The empty room.

Greyness. Silence.

The empty room.

A grandfather clock: tick *tack* tick *tack* tick *tack* tick *tack*.

— Why are you holding the door open? he asks.

She giggles.

— Why?

That smell. Her smell.

She giggles. — Go on, she says.

The clock: tick *tack* tick *tack* tick *tack* tick *tack*.

— You want me to go through? he asks.

She giggles.

— Do you?

She giggles.

He steps past her through the French windows.

And again the room.

And he stands at the window.

And the voice says: Everything passes. The good and the bad. The joy and the sorrow. Everything passes.

THE END